Veranda Man

Nicola Knox

Veranda Man

Acknowledgements

Many of these poems have appeared in publications such as
Social Alternatives, *School Magazine* NSW, *Tirra Lirra*, *fourW*,
Centoria and *Hecate*.

Over the years, I have enjoyed the help and friendships to be found
in a number of poetry groups. I thank them for supportive critiques
that have undoubtedly shaped my work.

Thanks also to my daughters Martha and Maria, for their often good
advice, and thanks again to my husband Peter
for his bracing optimism.

For Peter so many thanks

Veranda Man
ISBN 978 1 76041 169 5
Copyright © text Nicola Knox 2016
Cover photograph: *Whitegates*, by John Haly

First published 2016 by
GINNINDERRA PRESS
PO Box 3461 Port Adelaide 5015 Australia
www.ginninderrapress.com.au

Contents

Bernini's Fountain	7
Presbyterian Section	8
Outside the Chimpanzee Enclosure	9
Calculation	10
Tourist at Ming Mountain	11
Trapeze on a Bright Day	12
Strangler Vine	13
Storyteller	14
Defraction	15
Shame and Misfortune	16
Angelo and David	17
Veranda Man	18
Qana, 2006	19
Date Palm of Judea	20
Asylum Seekers and the Greater White Rhinoceros	21
Crow in the City	22
Erhu Violin, China	23
Centennial Park, 2003	24
Summer in the City, King's Cross	25
Monkey Mia, WA	26
Barnyard	27
Trains	29
Cockroach	30
New Moon on the Square	31
Found Bone	32
The Dreaming	33
Insomnia	34
By Stars and Moon	35
Melba Remastered	36
Butterfly in the Daintree Forest	37

Moving Air	38
Where River Meets Sea	39
Farmer's Song	40
Writing to a Detainee, 2004	41
Star Watchers for Pharaoh	42
Ladies Who Lunch	43
kangaroos at hungry head	44
Japanese Prints	45
Perspective	46
Gaelic Reading	47
Kalbarri Mouse	48
Sappho's Songs	49
Sorry	50
Goldfish and Salary Man	51
Sleepless in Limestone Country	52
Old Baldy	53
Journey	54
Upside Down Land	55
Nefertiti	56
St Paul's, Easter	57
Pinchgut	58
Fowlyard Kingdom	60
Yellow Waters Morning, Kakadu	62
Valla Beach, The Rock	63
Symposium	64
Scroll Painting: Sumida Bridge	65
Wind Farm, Esperance	66
Comet Dust	67

Bernini's Fountain

Bernini drowsing hot, hot afternoon
dreamed up a fountain and grotto
where water and shadow might meet.
Minimalist, he added one statue only
a slender Venus, well veiled, on her shell.
Pleased with the result, he sent drawings off
to the Pope, suggested His Holiness consider
possibilities of furnishing an empty square
with a fountain grander than any to date.
The Pope on vacation almost expiring
from boredom was delighted with the scribbles
commissioned Bernini on the spot.
Considering himself knowledgeable about art,
urged addition of novelties, perhaps a centaur
huge-thighed or Bacchus raising a goblet of gold.

Bernini sulked at the vulgarities he was obliged to add.
But when all was done he mingled with Roman artisans
housewives, aristocratic idlers, open-mouthed tourists
hearing their cries of delight at such a plentitude
of strange creatures, prancing, plashing rainbowed foam.
Thought grudgingly perhaps the Pope might be right.
His friends often hearing the sculptor's grumbles
now laughed at him, dabbling hands and feet in water
insisted he too must love the piece.

Presbyterian Section

Rim to curved rim
extend long plains
of fallow, ploughed lands
springing young wheat
life throbbing, rising, dying
renewed in each year's orderly round.
Our ancestors have chosen
to lie at last, fenced off
from the exuberant town
neat, decent in dour granite
crowned rarely with seraphim.
But always dates of birth, death,
who was beloved of whom,
chiselled in narrow straight lines
above bones waiting for covenanted days.

Outside the Chimpanzee Enclosure

Grave and still as ebony gods
they squat in the shrines
of ochre coloured walls
not sleeping but watchful
eyes bright as flint.
We lick ice cream, crunch,
slurp. Somebody reads aloud the sign:
Chimpanzees have been known to comprehend
seventy per cent of human conversation.
A juvenile uncurls from his shadowy space,
lopes to the wire mesh, begins to tear
a directory provided by Telstra.
Section A–K goes first: carries my name
my street, my town in a small disembowelling
by one who is learning pleasures of revenge.

Calculation

Making wind gusts visible
small birds sweep in
to reach our water tank
ring its overflow, a calculation
of wagtails, sparrows, silver eyes.

A rough magpie flashes down
scatters small birds like
so many ragged leaves
dips long beak, slaking thirst
then gives thanks, tuning sky
in intervals regular enough
to satisfy any Pythagorean.

Tourist at Ming Mountain

We have come down from Qin's great wall
thinking of how two thousand years ago
messages were smoked from tower to tower
reaching the emperor by noon, wolves' dung
best for signalling. Sit beneath the mountain now
and see how autumn, garnet coloured
coils woods of birch and ash.

Think also of conscripts, ordered into forest
at dawn, scouring for caked and frozen shit.
Still children, did they weep for mothers,
for steaming bowls of chicken broth. Summoned
by drum, how often red chilblained hands
hauled panniers uphill.

Harsh the buffeting by dragon winds
we can feel now, snarling from the east.

Trapeze on a Bright Day

Lycra sleek he flies across the blue
into sun's haloed eye
hangs for moments, swinging
with music, synthetic and slow.
On last lunge, catches rope
flings himself to a silvery ball
balances lightly, mothlike
bathed by gold of day's end.
We hold breath, a corporate breath,
exultant for him, fearful for this lord
of sky and sun and wind.

And, since we are human
what secret longing
for miscatch, missed step.

Strangler Vine

The small vine that grew
at fig tree base, twined slowly
year after year, round the trunk
in a friendship of sorts,
sharing sunshine, rainfall
the ministrations of birds.

Relentless growth
of the strangler vine
now an ossuary
holding the tree's remaining
few bones, all the springing life
withered, decayed, long ago.

Stumbling on this vine
in darkening afternoon,
remember those cathedrals
and abbeys where stone
encloses roofless space
shorn of believers and priests.
Sanctuary sought only
by day-blinded owls.

Storyteller

In the country sometimes,
when we were young,
skylarks sang out of sight
clear, driving notes of joy
down, down
from the sun's blind eye,
across ploughed lands
and paddocks of winter wheat.

On such days, swinging
on the front gate, in bright air,
you, being older, shared your learning
insisted that larks in exultation,
that is to say, in hosts, travelled
back and forth from far countries,
air flowing across chambered hollows
of their throats, effortless music
to enthral listeners on dull earth.

So many of the tales you told
what was true, what made up,
the magic of stories, to while away
days of holiday remembered still.

Defraction

Still waters dimple
when summer-idle boys
skim stones across the lake.

Governed by laws
of liquid surfaces, push
and pull of things struck

drops become waves
that circle wide and wider
to rock boats moored

on the tranquil far shore.
As random happenings
distort time's flow

down generations
the careless insult, the blow,
stones hurled by a shepherd boy,

become tanks at the city gates
revenge taken over and over
enemies never reconciled.

Shame and Misfortune

An evening of wine and cheese
to view neighbour's travel film
(taken by Tom, commentary by Mary.)

Such a shame, Venice, you can't believe
how much rubbish in the canals – those
guidebooks talking about spangled light
on water at sunset, all nonsense. Florence
was quite pretty but there was some church
outside our bedroom seemed to ring bells
all night, didn't get a wink. Now here's
the Eiffel Tower, move it up a little Tom.
We've never been so high. Was quite dizzy
for hours after. Shame the weather too.
No use having a camera in all that rain,
so nothing really of Paris. Food was OK
and at least you could rest your feet
in coffee shops. But my goodness, the price
for a teeny tiny cup. Last stop, London.
Tom got this great shot of Changing the Guard.
Pity though the Queen had gone off to Balmoral
the television said.

Have to say both Tom and I agree, travel
makes you realise how good it is to be an Aussie.

Angelo and David

Each morning in Florence, tumbrils
bring the evening's leavings to the morgue
before they go to the lime pits –
entertainment for home-going partygoers,
medical or the merely curious. Angelo is there
(hating death's smell and changing pallet of colours)
still searching for model hands to complete his David.

Today among bodies struck down in a brawl
hands strong, capable, long tapering fingers
right for one who might have been shepherd boy,
giant killer, musician, king.

But lips so tender, Angelo could have kissed them.

Veranda Man

Neighbours named him so
driving by in their tin Lizzies.
He never seemed to go anywhere
stretched summer and winter
on the veranda's sagging couch
his dusty wife seen only taking
eggs to market, cream to factory
in her gig. Their many children
appeared now and again at school
often without coats or shoes,
the father a public affront
lying plumply inert every day
passing time away as scotch thistles
and tumbleweed littered his land.

Returning years later I saw with curious sadness
that nothing remained of Veranda Man.
His land once so down-at-heel now
a shimmer of steel silos upright sheds
and paddocks pristine.

Looking back I wonder was his life tranquil
studying the continual change in clouds
watching them drive shadows across
his unhusbanded land, listening to sparrows
build nests in the veranda eaves?

Qana, 2006

believed to be site of the turning of water into wine

On a day of parching heat
at the wedding feast
wineskins ran dry
shaming the bride's family.

Christ's mother, knowing
her son's compassion,
asked could he help.
So it was courtesy as a guest

not holy purpose
drove him to change water
into wine. In Qana this year
when a kindness, a miracle

might have saved the city
water turned to blood
and flesh to fire
without a god in sight.

Date Palm of Judea

From a discarded seed in Masada a date palm has been grown

Longest day of a short life
he tried not to weep the years foregone
but still a hungry child was comforted by fruit
from his father's grove, ate slowly,
spitting out seeds, one by one
savouring a last pleasure before the march
the long march to the cliff edge.

Frightened brave boy, he could not know
that a memory of himself, like a shadow
in moonlight or a fragrance on wind
might be imagined centuries on
in a discarded seed's rebirth.

Asylum Seekers and the Greater White Rhinoceros

Thankfully he did not wake
tucked in his cave above the Java Sea.
He loves sleep even more than food,
and we have been careful not ever
to make sudden noises or disturbance
round the dear fellow.

When the boat arrived, filled with ragged souls
a natural concern for all of us that the wretched folk
and their crying children might cause serious trouble
for the Greater White, set his one horn to horrible glowing
preliminary to rage. We urged the boat's captain to turn around
advised there were many other islands, supplied a few loaves
milk, water, and so on: we have always been a kindly people.

In the end, rather forcibly, we have had to tow the wretches out
where they will certainly find a more suitable refuge.
With luck might even be picked up by nearby fishermen.
We do feel for them but we have an enormous responsibility
to maintain the well-being of our Greater White Rhinoceros.
All in all, things turn out mostly for the best.

Crow in the City

By the bus stop
there's a lone and dusty tree
where Crow sits, talking to himself
or scolding minions late for
an afternoon of pirating.
With that angry yellow eye
and cutlass of a beak
he's every inch a warrior
to the last glossy feather.

Now his voice changes
dropping to a grumble
maybe at city heat
nostalgic for farm dams
and winter paddocks
rich in carrion.

All at once Crow turns mendicant
and from the black pit of his throat
a wail, rising, falling, falling
Oh stand by me, stand by me
In this fading light, his feathers
seem rusty and his eyes are dull.

The only coin I can throw is pity
where he sits, lonely in that tree.

Erhu Violin, China

Lying in summer grass one thousand years ago
a youth, a music maker, tired from rehearsals
fell asleep, dreamt he was a butterfly
dipping, soaring, across limitless worlds
among a host of fragile creatures.
But one, most beautiful, wings folded high
came to rest upon his heart.

Waking he knew he must invent
an instrument fine enough
to call the pretty creature
from airy realms to live with him forever.
Disdained those drums, bells
and bamboo pipes that once delighted
now too rough and loud for wooing.
For months he worked upon a novelty
bringing sounds of wind in treetops
water down to valleys,
surely glad enough to entice
any butterfly. So Lady Erhu was born
long, long neck to hold taut
just two strings of purest silk
tied to a sound box of python string.
Sadly, butterfly life swift as a sigh.
His Concert Master brought some comfort
saying Lady Erhu herself would be the legend
as central voice in a great new opera:

Song for a thousand butterflies.
loved and played for the centuries.

Centennial Park, 2003

Refusing newspapers, radio, television
all rumours and threats of war
go this afternoon to sit by a pond
in the park: observe ducks, plump at peace
among reeds, while nestlings struggle
down a slope of sunlit lawn, their clumsy,
brave plop into water, downy wings outstretched
join an armada of proud mothers
among the circling ripples – brown birds
black, turquoise, green, tan, preening, diving.

Autumn sun lovers and parents
scold their young homewards.
Through the gathering dusk
a squadron of geese is flying
in long lines across a sunset-bannered sky.

Watching them you think of those
other flights, freighted with death
crossing deserts and mountains
searching out cities whose time has come.

Summer in the City, King's Cross

On the fruit stall by the station
cabbages grow pale, mangoes
and grapes begin to burst.
A golden-haired girl waits, droops
in the awning's shade, sandals
grown tight. Lone street sweeper
gathers up cigarette butts, syringes
dead leaves, from round languid feet.

Circling the fountain, like old men of Troy
the park's philosophers argue with themselves
setting out ancient truths, brilliant foretellings.
Brown-suited man sits on his milk crate
notebook and pens laid neatly beneath a sign
2 dollars one poem, five poems for three dollars
but summer heat has drained, it seems, all impulses
towards billets-doux.

There remains only a question: shall coffee
be taken in styrofoam, watching people move
through the orange smoked air of the street,
or shall we treat ourselves to a table,
dingy china cups, in the cafe of speechless shadows?

Monkey Mia, WA

Viridescent morning light
tourists come, rolling up
trouser legs, hitching skirts
to paddle frosty waves
vigilant for dolphins.

And in they tumble
round as submarines
black eyes fixed on creatures
packed shank to purpling shank.
Dolphins tickle toes, nibble knees
put on a flirty, flirty show
before breakfast of small fish.

Burping then, they throw a final wink
for camera flash and roister back to sea
no last look for sad adoring us.

Barnyard

All farms have them, dumping grounds
for dead machinery, ironmongery of dreams
rusted history half-buried in yellow grass
and purple thistles.

We went for a walk one afternoon
to settle long-running arguments
about that tree in the barnyard
carved by tomahawks for coolamon,
shield or boat or just hacked
by some idle farmhand.

This day a child rummaging
amongst old tyres and rusted machinery
found a wheel hub, painted silver.

That's from the buggy grandmother had
for going into town,

said an old uncle who knows all the stories,

she had two black-matched horses
and the gig was silver and bright green.
Pretty smart, lasted for years. Drove it
myself once or twice to school.

There's a cloud comes over the day
as elders think of that long ago pain and fear –
the little woman, smart in her town outfit
wheeling up to the house gate at sunset
getting down, quick and spry. But an errant hem
caught in the wheel, set horses to a panic bolt.
From what we have been told of her thrifty sense
she would have been the last to say,

break up the gig, shoot the horses.

Would have scolded to see that decay in the grass.

Trains

It was steam in those days,
unforgettable the cold
of a 4 a.m. wait for that long
curve of light to clatter
out of darkness.

Corridors and seats
jammed with young recruits
travelling north they said
always travelling north.
Even a prim schoolgirl could see
the fright in their eyes, the terror,
under drunken bluster, primed
by a stop at the station buffet.

Now, though steam's no more,
(coal dust coating hands and lip)
still the lingering whistle at black crossings
the fog wreathed lights of sad freight yards,
hope already dying: new start in a town
that has no welcome.

Cockroach

He ducks, he weaves
cunning as beast can be
and now I, poor, clumsy fool,
stumble behind in a rage
growing more murd'rous
each frantic second.

If I should succeed,
crushing bones beneath my foot
shovelling pathetic remains
to garbage bin, will I not be
an assassin, left to contemplate
this mindless destruction
of a creature whose radar sense
of enemy moves, matches sleek agility.

One cockroach in my kitchen today
tomorrow a thousand. So,
horrid creature, expect no mercy from me.

New Moon on the Square

Mice in lineal descent
from the first mice, dart
from house to old house
where veined hands bait
vengeful traps with cheese
or teepee twigs for meagre fires.
In verdigrised mirrors, widows
seek bride faces, sigh over
the tier of white cake
dried out, coffined in glass.
Then boil an egg, switch on telly.

But on the square
children still shout at ball
beneath an early moon.
Young men, Reebokked,
catatonic, pound the verge
and dogs break out from jail
crying saturnalia.

Mice, old brides, children, dogs
sport or dream this frosty dusk.
Time runs its course, so turn
a silver coin beneath the moon
and wish one day, one playtime more.

Found Bone

Out of newsday's radio horrors
one story comes clear: discovery
in some centuries' old rubbish tip,
of a lute carved from a crane's wing.

I have seen gold-brushed parchments
where these legendary birds of love,
spread wings across sunlit plains
in grave courtship dance.

And marvel now at how dead bone,
created from an ancient consummation
has come to live again on radio's agog.

The Dreaming

Around the cafe
where three roads meet
hang drifters. Idlers
longing to enter
knowing, but not for certain
that within are silken couches,
cascading fountains and girls
offering wine, voices sweet
away from the traffic's roar
(swirling from Darlo to the 'Loo.)
At each tired day's end
waiters in dingy black, put out
garbage, crash down the shutters
shut in malodour of a thousand feasts,
lock out dreamers sprawled at the door.

Insomnia

Like a child in tantrum
who's wept too long
the wind having gusted all day
sighs now, in long gasps.

Just before dusk closes
feel the breeze
swing from east to south
now a gentler climate

At midnight, there is a stirring
a new small wind, a whisper
of leaves against the window,
birds restless from the day
begin to stir themselves awake.
Now the old house is creaking
as if thieves crept from a far room
sensing not all souls sleep.
Hours yet before first cockcrow
calls up dawn.

By Stars and Moon

Sailors sometimes, like elver fish
and leaping trout, steer by stars.
Birds in flocks choose stellar light
to lead them home from icy peaks
or languid tropic lands.
But lovers love best the round
and silver moon when she
is at high lustre. Mayflies
dance through steamy night
and fall at last to fecund
passionate death.
Seahorses, enamoured, grapple
lunar hours deep on the ocean's floor.
And once a year, when moon
is quartered, coral implodes
enriching coasts faraway.

On such a night, on such a night
human lovers love the moon
scribbling, carving, on sea wall
park bench, small odes of pain
passion and sad betrayals –
Kate is a slut, Craig's a waste of space
love you a lot spunk

On such a night, on such a night
Dean lies in sand with Jess
until that blessed moon grows pale
and morning stars hang out to warn
that love must hurry on its way.

Melba Remastered

It's as if Persephone
was singing her way
from a wintery world
to her every springtime
on earth.

Ghost of the voice adored
by generations long gone
echoing, tinny, sad,
thin for so stout a lady
splendid in velvet and furs.

Our elders told such gossipy tales
admirers drinking wine from her
antipodean slipper: she sipping champagne
between curtain calls.
Bit of a handful, but oh to hear her Mimi,
said mother, devoted reader
of *Lady's Home Journal*.
Now Mimi returns, voice brittle,
crystal tapped by fingernails
in discreet applause.
But gone the dark eyes,
glorious throat, gone the goblets
of wine, long withered are roses
and lovers all forgotten.
Now remains only faint music
from a robotic throat.

Butterfly in the Daintree Forest

We were promised butterflies
four colours blue, amber
jade and black. So far
this long drowsy afternoon
one only, white flecked with green
dancing just above the forest floor
where chequered sunlight falls.

One minute ago sudden small winds
whipped her halfway up the strangler vine.
Now she rests on the veranda rail
in an important raising of wings
preening as if it was her derring-do
set all the treetops nodding
like kings in conference.

Moving Air

In the last hour before sunset
observe how air is rarely still
stirring trees to caesura
a sudden spin of leaves
curved like tiny scimitars
on corkscrewing breeze

over and over wings quicken
the hot smoky light,
small birds seeking gnats,
cabbage moths, late butterflies,
even the kookaburra
coloured like stringy bark
believing himself motionless
invisible cannot control
the flutter of one feather
fails to paralyse with his stare
the gecko whisking faster
than light out of death's range
safe into leaves that barely stir
beneath the farmyard gate.

Where River Meets Sea

When the river
the Murchison
flows out from
high rampart walls
to meet the sea
there is dropped
a child's ball
bright red
once loved
now lost
it loiters
at ocean edge
tossing forward
dragged back
on each wave.
Fears perhaps
that it might
be carried on
a lonely voyage
to the far side,

to India.

Farmer's Song

Mile upon mile
no hindrance to the eye
air luminous, without sun
yet clear. Sound runs anvil sharp
ewe call to lamb, plover keening
for its mate. Day grows indigo,
neighbour comes to borrow
our new set of harrows.
We drink tea hot and sweet
talk of bumper crops, cattle sleek
and sheep so heavy in wool
shearers will cry: penalty pay.

Is this the year at last
to tell the banker
where to put it.

Writing to a Detainee, 2004

You a character
in a story of unkindness
words crossing, recrossing
barren space, stilted language
chosen from dictionaries: Farsi, English
little more substance
than rain-scribbles on
autumn leaves.

Yesterday an email came
sudden, abrupt, frightened.
I reply. Today my screen alerts
message cannot be received.

You exist, existed
as a shape once, electrifying air.
Now my conscience must bear
the incredible weight
of your going, your fear.

Star Watchers for Pharaoh

Were they lonely
those watchers on towers,
raiding heaven night after night
recording comet tracks
conjugating rise and fall of planets
explosions and fallout of stars
how shadows shifted
in a year's diurnal round:
the minute, the second
in every year,
when a kingly tomb
might be bathed in light

Through a lifetime
of night vigils, fitful day-sleep
watchers forgot speech
handed data to engineers
without discussion or greeting.
Inarticulate in a land of talkers
and tellers of stories,
they were given hardly a thought.
But once a poet called them
shepherds of heaven and a pharaoh
had his faithful servant carved
in very small effigy at the foot
of the royal sarcophagus
showing the watcher beneath
a burst of star signs, sleeping at last.

Ladies Who Lunch

My neighbour's five hens are coming through
the broken fence, high-stepping single file
red combs worn like tiny fascinators
for these are stylish fowl, older matrons all.

The leader, a plump Rhode Island Red
halts at seeing me: gives a polite cluck-cluck
then urges her Black Orpingtons on to where
snails and worms lie beneath the lemon tree.

Elegance must be dropped when these ladies
furrow soil with boney legs. But they swallow
each juicy morsel in meditative way of gourmets
afterwards stroll to where sun warms the mint bed.

Pretending to ignore me they lower themselves
raise wings like languid fans. The leader turns
head into shoulder, draws up pink eyelids
preparing for a discreet nap before going home.

Suddenly, a flurry of tut-tuts, squawks,
shrieks even, beady eyes staring into the sky.
I think, eagle at least. No. Simply cloud crossing sun
a scurry, a hurry to the fence, gentility offended

hostess forgotten, unfarewelled.

kangaroos at hungry head

reading by lamplight
of minoans their gods
and opium ecstasies
fall asleep at last
wake at dawn to see
faint shapes   grey on grey
moving through mist
and pillared eucalypts

at the treeline they halt
these silent priests heads
hands perfectly at prayer
waiting for the first
brazen spears of sun
to scatter all demons
of labyrinthine night

Japanese Prints

Itahana Station
Many steps still
up to snow-hut,
white cloaks,
white hats.
Everyone silent
under black leaves
stiff with ice.
Who sees the red sky.
Full Blossom At Arashiyama
Petals drift water.
Dreamy poets almost miss last
call from the ferry.
Boatmen cursing, pole back
on the dark'ning river
lamps already lit.
Fragrance of flowers
everywhere. No music
who dares sing
or even speak across
the boatman's rage.
Poem of Funyia
A dark journey for
frightened women poling
their high-prowed boat
among poison green
lilies, deep curves of water.
Turbanned and huge
magician sits at boat's centre,
face masked, commanding all.

Perspective

After lunch an uncertain time
the master's cheeks often high-coloured
and morning's serious work
of droned multiplication tables,
dictation, all considered done.
If Sir was in jovial mood
it would be pictures shown from the *Art Book*
stories, even poems, read to us, allowing
possibilities of gazing across the yellow
emptiness of paddocks to the railway station,
its faint promise of escape to cities or seaside.

But if his day had darkened, we knew
by the snapping of chalk in half
that each child would be called out,
to demonstrate something called *Perspective*
a puzzling word still associated with knuckles rapped,
chalk snatched from clumsy fingers, thrown at heads.

Last journey of return, the schoolhouse was gone
and in its place a widened road of bitumen
landscaped with trees on either side, converging
across the plain to a single point:
long ago lessons comprehended at last.

Gaelic Reading

Yesterday I heard a poet reading
from the Gaelic, a tongue incomprehensible
a language peat dark, strong as cromlech
heavy with lament, opening portals in the blood.

Not remembered until now
the blackthorn stick stored
in my uncle's barn, supposed
to be carried by grandfather
brave boy who cut it green
in a springtime on the very day
he left Ireland and home.
As a child I longed for that wood
to bloom like the saint's staff
in old legend, told by Aunty Louise
the burr of her voice reflecting voices
of the *old country* from which grandfather came.

I knew him only in remembrances
of how he built a farm out of strange rough land,
buried two wives, raised god-fearing children
but always, they said sorrowing for home,
for the old voices, the old ways.

Kalbarri Mouse

The desert mouse
knows no colour
but palest grey
of moonlight
suffusing stones
and spinifex.

Venturing
from silent caverns
of his house
only after dark
this troglodyte
of a mouse hears
night after night
commotion of lives
curlews
long flights of geese
calling, plaintive on wind.

Suddenly the terrible sound
of human footfall, crashing all
in its path, halts the ducking,
weaving, busy way
of Kalbarri Mouse
as he flees his destiny.

Sappho's Songs

In those days there was profit
to be made in the use and reuse
of papyrus for packing vases, wine jars.
Schoolmasters, being frugal
taught the young how to write verso
across discarded recto drafts.
Much old papyrus even shipped back
to Egypt for bandaging of noble bodies.
So fragments of Sappho's sweet songs
were found like precious stones hidden,
glowing, in musty wrappings of the dull dead.
Words faded, smudged, lost
but enough of delight, love and grief
to know that we would not give up this meagre hoard

for all the golden crowns and armies of Lydia.

Sorry

Plumb in the middle of father's best paddock,
in all the seasons he had known, ploughed over
sown, let go to grass, a midden remained
stubborn and charcoal grey, coloured by centuries.
We learnt from *The Fourth Grade Reader*
that middens were made by people who roamed
an untended country until white settlers
tidied up, fenced off waterholes,
populating land with cattle, sheep
warned off poachers (always black.)

As children we had our own picnics
in swampy bush not far from the midden
near a mud-brick house built by a long gone
family. Now this was crumbling into itself.
But we could still finger the holes
once bored to hold guns aimed
at natives, hostile probably, perhaps curious.
No time when you're being surrounded by blacks
to question whether they meant to murder you or not
better safe than sorry Dad would tell us.

As for that midden, last time I talked to the farmer
who took over, he says that for all those years of ploughing
and sowing, years of drought and sudden floods
the midden remained. And nowadays nobody
is allowed to touch the thing.

Part of this sorry business, I suppose

Goldfish and Salary Man

In a tank of fish
he sees a gold minnow
among huge creatures
small, misplaced
pop-eyes reflecting misery
rosy mouth gasping
against glass: my mouth
he thinks, its soundless cries
of despair and misery,
salary man perpetually
in a pod of sharks.

Sleepless in Limestone Country

Tonight the house, stone-walled, solid,
long-rooted in earth seems a flimsy thing
as stars roar over its roof beams
some like glittering, precious stones,
some sweeping in pale fumes of the Milky Way.

Sleep does not come
though the calls of plovers
sheep, even barking dogs, reassure.

Such a cracking and creaking
of dried out wood, loosening bricks
a perpetual dragging down
to the country's dark heart,
its honeycomb caverns and shores
of stalactite lakes where gargantuan
creatures once scattered their bones

Looking out across neat vineyards,
the folded volcanic hills lit only
by truckers' headlights,
my restless mind grows drowsy
thinking of lives and galaxies
still to be revealed.

Old Baldy

Old horse we half-loved, half-despised
on frost bright mornings cajoling him to life,
pulled up from crackling grass,
led about with curses, small thwacks
fed warm mash, a sparse kindness
before we trailed our bikes to school.

His sad milky eyes looked blankly
on the scowls, impatient care
doled out in return for years of safe haulage
through heat and dust, wind and rain.

Took all morning for him to move away
from the hay shed wall, until at noon
bathed in the sun's full warmth
he would break into a canter,
almost a gallop of joy, once round the paddock.
Grandfather, looking from the kitchen window
says, *Old fellow I know how it is*
taking time each morning to get up,
testing legs, stretching away stiffness
ready for the day ahead.

Journey

Midday and still he has
last checks to make:
machinery tarpaulined,
a sick beast well sheltered,
growth of new planted seedlings.

Returns with a moth, cupped
in work-worn hands always able
to soothe creatures out of a panic.
*You don't often see her sort in daylight
such a beauty,* he says

spreading the crimson wings, so that
I too can delight in a novelty. Together
we place her in a bush by the door.
For a moment, uncertain, she trembles
then lifts on a rising breeze

He sighs, remembering day is half over
and still the journey to make
after all the courtesies of goodbye.
We feel ache in the words
Back before cropping I reckon

Upside Down Land

...when swans were black and eagles white, bees did not sting and mammals laid eggs, trees kept their leaves but shed their bark... (J. Martin in 1930s, quoted by National Museum of Australia)

Charles Sturt dreaming of hidden seas
trudged deserts, dragging a whale boat
into a land of ever vanishing mirage
while his crew grew, day by day
gaunt as phantom sailors.
Afterwards the preachers
earnest Lutherans called by God
tramping ochre coloured mile on mile,
rising from camp each morning, trim
in shirt fronts, ties and trilby hats. Goal:
saving heathens, who drifted off
when flour and sugar gave out
exclaiming in wonder among themselves
at strangeness of newcomers.

Down the track from Darwin
where tumbleweed blows
and termite hills rise in vicious peaks
there stands a hotel of plastered brick
grand with plate glass, lakes dug
for sailing, swimming, resort pleasures.
Drained of water over night it's said,
a mystery of drought, famished aquifers
or simply country not to be bridled,
where withered men sit on sun-baked
verandas, telling all within hearing
of the dreams that have set them adrift
in best left alone land.

Nefertiti

Loveliest girl of Thebes
no wonder she became
pride of Pharoah's court
serene above the quarrels
of eunuchs, priests
oblivious to all struggles for place.
outshining timid foreign princesses,
she went with the king
to a strange new town (from which all gods
save the Sun itself, were banished.)

After the first years in that desert place
Pharoah grew addled from, it was whispered,
too much praying in midday heat.
Nefertiti began to replace her husband
at audiences in the Great Throne Room
a frightening change to sacred custom.
Only the highest could receive ambassadors and judges.

One morning the Royal Steward found her gone.
disappeared like a wraith imagined. Not for her
a gold packed tomb, the ceremonials
of entering the Next World.

Was it a swift death, thrown to crocodiles,
customary end for troublemakers. Or, maybe
lying somewhere buried in sand
a bundle of dismembered bones.
Lost daughter of Thebes
loveliest girl of her day.

St Paul's, Easter

Morning floods the golden tulip cups
bright as vessels of sacramental wine.
Day peals out commands that rock
the steeple top   *go, go, get you to a prayer*

Picking up their blankets from the holy steps,
blinking in the shrilling, chilling sun.

Mister, lady just two pounds
cup of coffee, cigarettes

Hours are broken into pieces
fat promises that wafer on the tongue
Need just enough for bus ride to the hospital

Time spends itself in fields and fields
of candles, flowering for the worthy dead.
Ragged man cast out – sings sweet and faint

baby is a'tellin' me, nearly time to go.

Pinchgut

Mrs Macquarie sat in a sandstone chair
looking contentedly out on the harbour,
botany book open on her lap: strange
she thought, haymaking on her father's farm
must be almost done, while here
on a golden day, still winter. Now
watching an East Indiaman gliding by
sails furled, she was happy,
knowing plants and seeds for her garden
were in its hold.

White furrows in the ship's wake settling,
she glanced idly towards that rocky island,
curse of mariners for where it stood, right
in the centre of shipping lanes. But pretty
she thought, seeing it glow
in afternoon light. And the coats
of soldiers tying up small boats to the
out-crop's wharf, were a brilliant scarlet
even from this distance. Today she
should really have brought a paintbox.

But in the soldiers' midst, Elizabeth could see
two struggling men being dragged towards
some sort of platform raised under a scraggly tree.
Paralysed with horror she could not look away
as the victims jerked up to swing violently
in a south wind turned suddenly ice-cold.

Afterwards, by order of the Governor
all hangings, floggings and so on
to be conducted out of decent peoples' sight.
Harbour views must be kept unsullied,
already highly valued.

Fowlyard Kingdom

Painter of pet animals
for Amsterdam's new rich
Melchior d'Hondecourt loved
commissions to immortalise poultry.
A colleague once said (only partly
in jest) that hens surrounded by chicks
when painted by Melchior
resembled Madonnas.
Another friend invited to dinner
brought along, a glossy red cock bird,
saying roast it or paint it he will go well
either way. Melchior, struck by the rooster's
commanding eye, saw him as a sergeant major,
protective where skittish pullets were concerned
but also an educator for his harem, teaching
hens to stand side on, plump themselves
to a grassy verge or bend heads in demure fashion.
Melchior regarded the rooster as his companion
and it was often noted that the pair travelled
to the countryside, with Chanticleer carried
in a small chair strapped to the artist's back.
These trips resulted in charming rural backgrounds
for which the artist was famous.

Time passing, Melchior saw with concern
that his friend was becoming stiff with age.
He searched, and found, a likely companion
for the old rooster in a smart young fellow,
black-tailed, shiny-eyed, intelligent enough
to be trained in hierarchies of the fowl yard.
The morning after the new rooster's arrival
a strange cock-a-doodle wakened the household.
Melchior hurried to see results of his care
and affection. Alas!
Standing over the body of his friend
was the youngster preening opulent feathers
with a show-off look to nervously clucking hens.

Nothing for it but a burial with incense
and prayers. Melchior also placed a tiny sedan chair
upon the grave, a shrine to be picked over
by indifferent fowl.

Yellow Waters Morning, Kakadu

for St Francis

From bird to bird clear as glass
green song runs, circling earth
its billion, billionth dawn. Sun rises
above the marsh, first sun
first light, like Eden's morning.
Magpie geese in grave platoons
divide a dying moon, disappearing
into a still grey west. But here
above our heads, such belling
piping, whistling, as each creature
takes up its daily task: to live
to prey on, be preyed upon.
See the the bird as if silk brushed,
red stilts for legs, beak curved
walks water, ravishing lily cups
while ibis stalk lizards and frogs. Pied birds
having woken day in a concert of flutes
fall silent now, intent on robbing nests,
the homes of honey ants.
And crocodiles, log still, watch
with yellow eyes, for any fish or bird
or human coming their way.

Valla Beach, The Rock

Why this place and not another
hillock grown to mountain
from ocean's leavings: sea wrack
withy vines, small pebbles, shells
adrift on centuries of foaming tides.

What chance brought me
and not another
to see a standing stone
alchemised in evening sea light.

Symposium

Before wine goes in at the mouth
consider colour: sometimes
pale gold of barley or purple
as an evening sea. And all the range
of red between rose and crimson.
Then there is that first scent of flavour
sometimes indifferent, mostly pleasant
and, too rarely, divine.
Now roll gently upon the tongue
so that serious drinking may begin.

But no more than three goblets!
We are warned that more and
goatish Dionysus takes over
especially if the wine is unwatered
slaves being lazy in these slipshod days.
Indeed there are gross hosts who
prefer to drink this way, caring nothing
for our meticulous rituals of mixing
and measuring in sculptured bowls.

But strangely, after each distinguished
sober affair at my table, wit and wine
flowing together it is difficult to recall
all the epigrams, the wise anecdotes,
the new lyrics. One must rely, dear friend
on the general flavour, the bouquet
so to speak, to recall the excellence
of our meetings

Scroll Painting: Sumida Bridge

Such a thrusting and tumult
crossing the bridge this bright spring day
smart young blades with high-piled hair
hunting in packs, dodging porters, parasols.
Children tumble, roar, their nurses scold
and kiss, sideways glance at knight passing.
But he, bold samurai, seeks only lady
in her curtained chair.

Boatmen row swift, racing
beneath the teeming bridge
first into Edo where houses
crammed like toys on green lawns
welcome promenaders home.

Wind Farm, Esperance

How to farm the wind
as kindly Aeolus did,
gathering gales
in sacks
releasing them
to blow
heroes home
from long wars
or in smaller gusts
help winnowers
sort grain from chaff
upon the harvest floor
Now, circling cliffs
thin windmills
with shiva arms
bend acre
upon acre
of green air
to do our will.

Comet Dust

It is not in configurations of heaven
that the stories of our lives are read
but in wreckage of galaxies
starry bones of comets falling, by chance
into seas of a passing planet.
Out of such a churning soup
it may be that star stuff transmuted
through aeons of accident
to plankton, ferns, birds
both winged and flightless
elephants, baboons and finally
creatures two-legged, upright
heads crammed with intricacies
sometimes loving
often murderous.

We have come so far
yet observing the light
that flows to this world
from stars forever dying
there are wonders, stories
still to unfold.

www.ingramcontent.com/pod-product-compliance
Lightning Source LLC
Chambersburg PA
CBHW062158100526
44589CB00014B/1866